ANDREA RAYNOR

REFLECTIONS OF GRACE

═ FINDING HOPE AT GROUND ZERO ═

ATRIA BOOKS

New York   London   Toronto   Sydney   New Delhi

ATRIA
BOOKS

An Imprint of Simon & Schuster, Inc.
1230 Avenue of the Americas
New York, NY 10020

First Atria Books ebook edition September 2021

ATRIA BOOKS and colophon are trademarks of Simon & Schuster, Inc.

The Simon & Schuster Speakers Bureau can bring authors to your live event. For
more information or to book an event contact the Simon & Schuster Speakers
Bureau at 1-866-248-3049 or visit our website at www.simonspeakers.com.

ISBN 978-1-6680-0118-9

In memory and honor of the Foley brothers,
Tommy and Danny
FDNY Rescue Company 3
Heroes of 9/11

CONTENTS

INTRODUCTION

GROUND ZERO TWENTY YEARS LATER

THE DUST HAS LONG cleared and any evidence of destruction has been swept away. A new tower rises like a defiant phoenix brushing the sky, yet something remains. Echoes. Echoes of what was.

Today this sacred ground shimmers with defiant rebirth. Once cradling the World Trade Center, the Twin Towers, and (sadly) Ground Zero, the site has reconfigured and risen again as One World Trade Center (the Freedom Tower) and the 9/11 Memorial and Museum. The breeze now carries, not the ashes of destruction or the stench of decay, but rather the fine mist of the reflecting pools. Listen, and you may hear the distant music of laughter, of casual conversations, of the bustle of meetings, and I'll-be-home-for-dinners. These echoes of life do not include being afraid to go to work or board an airplane. They are part of what *was*, namely life before September 11,

2001, and they remain a part of us. Those old enough to remember carry them in our cell memory.

In the immediate aftermath of the attack on the World Trade Center, I felt a strong sense of calling to volunteer at Ground Zero. I had been working as a hospice chaplain for several years and was well acquainted with death. What became imminently clear, however, is that nothing could have prepared me (perhaps any of us) for this task. If preparation was not a prerequisite for service, a leap of faith and a deep breath for courage certainly were. Those with whom I walked and served—firefighters, police, EMTs, volunteers, construction workers, food servers, mental health professionals, and fellow chaplains—embodied that courage and more. Some were driven by faithful friendship to the fallen or by steadfast promises made to their families. Some felt compelled to serve because they loved their city, a city groaning and in tatters. Some were following the call of the Divine. And others showed up simply because they knew they had the strength to do so.

Working at Ground Zero meant shouldering the responsibility of standing in for a wounded and grieving nation—for families desperate to dig barehanded into the rubble in search of their loved ones, for those crying out to a God who might dare explain *why*, for children missing their parents, for the unborn who would never know their fathers, and for the dead waiting to be found. Because I was there as a chaplain, I also felt a sacred duty to comfort and to pray for those who worked without ceasing on that shifting, sometimes perilous, always painful site. I committed to memory the tender moments that passed between strangers and gently carried in my heart the people whose bodies I blessed at the morgue. I wanted to reassure myself (and others) that the Divine was alive and ever present at Ground Zero, despite the smoldering mountain of evidence to the contrary.

Much was shattered on September 11, to be sure, but some things were not completely destroyed. They *could* not be destroyed. Goodness. Hope. Faith in the future. Reverence for life. Love. These virtues survived against all odds, and they continue to guide us toward deeper healing. The scars of 9/11 are a reminder of everything we lost—cherished loved ones, the safety we took for granted, dreams and images free of burning towers and people falling—but they also bear witness to our ability to survive and to face the unthinkable. Our spiritual and emotional scars point to the resilience of the human spirit and to the strength of living in community. They mark where we were wounded, yes, but also how we managed to stitch ourselves together. They are evidence of strength as well as pain.

What happened in the aftermath of the attacks on that September day was an extraordinary outpouring of compassion, empathy, and support. And for a few shining moments, we were united in our common humanity rather than clawing at each other's throats because of our differences. At Ground Zero, the response to the devastation was not a clenched fist. It was an outstretched hand. It was not revenge; it was shared heartbreak. Maybe those same strong hands formed their fists later. I'm not saying they didn't. But for a time, they were open and ready to help.

The profound determination and spiritual stamina of those I met at Ground Zero will remain etched on my heart. And surrounding all of us, inspiring all of us, compelling all of us was the silent presence of each person waiting to be found. The awareness of their presence inspired a reverence that is difficult to describe. It gave us strength and kept us moving. The living kept watch over the dead, while the dead kept company with the living. It was an unspoken agreement, one that required extraordinary patience and care. Sorrow permeated the air, but it was not oppressive. It was infused with love and love made it light. Because of this, with every shift and every pause to lend an ear, I found more than sorrow: I found hope.

At first the hope was, of course, to find survivors. Hope against hope. Even when it became clear that no one would be pulled alive from the rubble, the hope sustaining and energizing Ground Zero was not dashed. Not completely. Instead, it absorbed the blow, wobbled, and changed forms. It became focused on finding and reclaiming the lost. Each time a body (or body part) was recovered, hope beat its fragile wings. Initially, our hope was simply to help. After a while, we hoped to keep our spirits alive, to retain our faith in humanity, to not shut down. Some hoped their marriages would survive or their health would hold out. Others hoped to retire when the work was done. The unspoken hope of some was that they, too, would be remembered if the roles were ever reversed. Like countless others, I carried ashes home on my shoes and in my hair. I carried toxins in my body—but hope carried me.

In hope, we gathered the shattered pieces of those who

died. We gathered ourselves. With these pieces, we created a delicate stained-glass window through which the light could shine. We tried to mend the broken places with love, the cracks with gold. This helped us remember the presence of beauty in the midst of the destruction. Holding on to the hope that life mattered, that what we were doing mattered, strengthened our resolve.

Through the years, whenever I have spoken about my service as a chaplain to the morgue at Ground Zero, many have been surprised (and heartened) to learn that every part of every person received a blessing. It is a tender and sacred part of the story of 9/11. As more years passed, I feared this chapter would be lost unless shared once more.

Here you will find echoes of life at Ground Zero, stories of everyday people who found themselves called to face the unthinkable in that particular moment in time. They climbed the pile, they descended into the pit, they searched the rubble; they refused to give up. Some later succumbed to illnesses related to their service. Most still bear the scars. These are but a thimbleful of the stories and people of Ground Zero. I invite you to walk with them, and with me, as we remember.

GETTING THERE

Like most people, I can remember exactly where I was on September 11, 2001. I was in the middle of morning update at the Jansen Memorial Hospice in Tuckahoe, New York, where I served as chaplain and pastoral care coordinator. Each morning, at 8:30, we would gather to hear the report from the night before, learning who had died, who had had difficulty in the night, and who was currently in distress. Based on the report, we would triage, form our plans for the day, and then begin to move out into the community to care for the patients and families in our program.

In the midst of this familiar routine, our office manager, Evelyn, rushed in to inform us that a plane had hit the World Trade Center. We were stunned but assumed it to be a small private plane, one that had wandered off course. "Keep us posted," we told Evelyn with concern; then we went on with the report. Fifteen minutes later, she rushed in again, saying, "Another plane just hit the other tower!"

"Oh my God," said one of the social workers, "we're at war."

I remember thinking that this was a bit dramatic, but everything started spinning. We didn't have access to a TV, so we told Evelyn to bring in the radio. I ran to my desk to call my husband, who happened to be home that morning, and told him to turn on the television. I also instinctively called my parents in Indiana to let them know I was okay. I knew they would worry, even though I worked in Westchester, a good thirty minutes from the World Trade Center. My mother was relieved to hear my voice. "I knew you probably wouldn't be in the city this morning, but I'm so glad to hear from you." I could feel her concern and the fears with which she quietly struggles over having a child so far away, especially in this increasingly unpredictable world.

"I'm okay, Mom," I said. "I knew you would be worried. I'd better go, but I'll call you later."

I returned to the conference room, where the hospice team was listening to the radio and starting to form an emergency plan. This was before the towers fell, before we could grasp the scope of the nightmare. The patients who most needed to be seen would be seen. Those who could wait, or who could manage with a phone call, would be put off until tomorrow. After those with the most acute needs were attended to, all team members were to report back to the office. The thinking was that we should be ready to lend support to the local hospital. In those first hours, we fully anticipated a flood of wounded people coming in through the Lawrence Hospital emergency room in Bronxville, New York. Lawrence would be one of the closest Westchester hospitals available in the event that the city hospitals were overrun. And so we waited.

The towers fell. My husband watched in horror as the unthinkable transpired on the television. He said he was screaming as the first tower collapsed—and again as the second one folded like a house of cards. Then he rode his bike to one of the piers in Rye, where he could see the smoke billowing from across Long Island Sound. I paced the office ten miles away, torn between professional commitment and maternal instinct. I was prepared to assist with the wounded and dying, and felt called to do so if necessary, but I was also fighting a frantic desire to gather my children to me, to feel them and smell them and make sure they were safe. I thought of my mother—and, of course, I thought of the mothers who would not get a call, the ones who would be waiting and waiting for the dear voice that would never come. Finally, just before 3:00, I got in my car and headed back up to Rye. I knew there were clergy of every denomination within walking distance of the local hospital. And, as it would turn out, no wounded ever came.

I arrived at my children's elementary school just in time for pickup. Mothers were standing on the playground quietly asking about each other's husbands. Some were crying, others embracing. Everyone was trying to confirm whose husband worked in or near the towers and whose did not. The school had decided not to tell the children anything about the attack.

The prevailing wisdom was that parents should have the opportunity to explain it to their own children.

That evening, planes circled endlessly overhead. They roared over our house in loud bursts. I didn't know whether to feel protected or scared out of my mind. My husband and I sat with our two children, ages five and eight, to discuss what had happened. They nodded solemnly, clearly unable to grasp it. Who of us could? All of us were reaching for straws, for anything that might make sense of this heinously senseless act. Thinking it might help, we asked our eight-year-old daughter if she wanted to stay up with us and watch President Bush's first address to the nation. We thought she might find comfort in seeing that the country was not in chaos, and that someone was in charge. But when we asked her if she wanted to do this, she looked up at us earnestly and said, "But Mommy, we think President Bush is an idiot."

I stammered a bit and managed to explain, "Well, uh, yes, we don't agree with most of his policies, but he is in charge right now, and we need to pray for him. We need to pray that God gives him the wisdom to lead our country through this terrible time."

She nodded in agreement. "Okay, Mommy. I can do that. Let's watch."

Later that night, a loud explosion woke my husband and me out of a deep sleep. It sounded very near and very devastating. My husband bolted out of bed yelling, "Get the kids! Get the kids! They've bombed the city! We've got to get out of here!"

"Wait a minute," I said, grabbing him. "I think it was

thunder. Is it raining? Don't wake the kids yet. Turn on the television—or better yet, call the police department and see what they say."

He ran downstairs, turned on the TV, but didn't wait before calling the local police. I stood frozen in the dark hallway between our children's rooms, straining my ears for the sound of sirens or the reassuring rumble of simple thunder. Instead, I heard my husband hang up the phone, and by his slow, weary steps, I knew what he would report. He said that it was in fact thunder; the police told him that several other people had called thinking the same thing. *Thank God we didn't wake the kids,* I thought. Still, both of us were shaking as we lay silent in the darkness listening to the rain.

Two weeks later, I was sitting in my daughter's third-grade classroom at Back to School Night. Life was going on, but not exactly as usual. Everything was subdued and slightly surreal. Sixteen people had died in our small town of Rye, yet kids needed to go to school, people needed to go to work, and the routines of the living had to continue. Next to me that night was the mother of one of my daughter's classmates. As we began to talk, I said to her, "Wait a minute! Are you the bishop's wife?"

"Yes!" she told me with a smile. "And you must be the chaplain."

Earlier in the week, I had been helping out at a Girl Scout meeting when a little girl named Clara had informed me that her father was some sort of bishop. She was not nearly as impressed as I was. Apparently she and my daughter had been talking and made the discovery that both of them had clergy parents. Clara could not tell me what kind of bishop he was, or what denomination, but I was intrigued.

Now I found myself sitting next to her mother, the bishop's wife, Brook Packard. We laughed at how our daughters had found each other. Then our discussion quickly turned to the attacks on September 11. Brook told me that her husband, George, was the Episcopal bishop to the armed forces. He (and she) had gone to Ground Zero immediately after the attacks, and now George was directly involved in gathering clergy for service there. I told Brook about my background with hospice, with the dying and the dead, with grief and crisis intervention, and asked her to let the bishop know that I would be willing to help if needed. She seemed genuine when she thanked me, but she also informed me that he had been inundated with calls from clergy making the same offer. "But I'll let him know," Brook said, squeezing my hand.

About a week later, Bishop Packard called and said that he might need someone to fill a shift at Ground Zero. It was his shift, but he was scheduled to go to California that night. He wasn't promising anything, but he suggested we meet to talk about it. The only time he had was on Saturday morning while his daughter was playing soccer. We decided to look for each other at the game. It occurred to me as I headed onto the soccer fields that I had no idea what this man looked like. His daughter, like mine, played recreational soccer, which meant that there were at least half a dozen games going on at once, on small fields that blended together. There would be sidelines jammed with parents and brothers and sisters, with dogs and babysitters, and bigger children waiting their turn to play. There would be a line at the ice cream truck, and there would be no flashing sign over anybody's head saying, "September 11. September 11. Sign up here."

As I started across the field, however, I spotted him immediately. I later joked that he had that "holy air" about him, that bishop thing, but it really was the truth. He was walking about thirty yards ahead of me, hands behind his back, head inclined toward the ground. Even dressed in jeans and a casual shirt, moving in a sea of other parents, he was clearly the bishop. I had no doubt. When he lifted his eyes, I could see in them the weary wisdom of one who has endured much, and I felt in my own chest the resonance of a heart broken from bearing the weighty grief of others.

"George?" I said, as I approached him.

"Yes, hi." He smiled, slightly startled.

We stood and talked as the children played. I told him a little about myself, but I knew that the words were secondary to what he was seeking—a feeling, an impression. Could I be trusted with this task? Was I the right person to send in his place tonight? He said he would call if he needed me. I felt grateful just to have met him.

Around six o'clock that evening, the phone rang, and George asked if I could take his shift for the night—midnight to 8:00 AM. I said I would be honored. We made arrangements for him to stop by my house to give me instructions and identification. He told me over the phone to wear my collar and anything else that might identify me as clergy—a stole, a badge, anything. After some effort, I managed to dig up the clergy collar that I seldom wear. It's something I have never been very comfortable with. Perhaps it's because, where I come from in Ohio, Methodist ministers never wear them, or maybe I'm still not used to the curious stares I receive when I don it. In fact, one of the things I loved about being a hospice chaplain is that I had an excuse for not wearing the collar. I worked with people of all faiths, and I honored that by not dressing in something representative of one particular point of view.

What I soon came to realize, however, was how helpful the collar was at Ground Zero. There, it identified me; it set me apart from the civilian volunteers, from the Red Cross and the Salvation Army. It invited particular kinds of conversation; it offered comfort. It preceded me like a town crier, shouting, "In spite of what you see before you, God is here! God has not forgotten! God has the nerve to show up in all shapes and sizes and colors. Tonight God appears as a woman with long hair and a clergy collar. Go figure."

Bishop Packard knew that I would need everything I had to get me past the security checkpoints. The organization of pastoral care efforts at Ground Zero was still rather chaotic. The well-meaning and the simply curious were finding their way onto the site, some gawking, others proselytizing. Security was getting necessarily tighter, and therefore harder to penetrate, even for those who were authorized. I knew the other unspoken concern was the fact that I am a woman, and do not exactly look the part of a priest.

When the bishop arrived at my house, he offered me his field stole, his hard hat, and a paper mask. He also gave me an Episcopal chaplain's pin, an ID badge, the cell phone numbers of various priests who could help if I ran into trouble, instructions on where to go and how to get there, and he offered a prayer. I remember looking into his eyes as he was talking to me and thinking, *If this man trusts me with this task, then by the grace of God, I can do it.*

Before leaving, Bishop Packard enfolded my husband and me in an embrace. Our children were upstairs, and the three of us stood in the quiet of the living room with our arms around one another. I don't remember the words he said, but I remember the feeling of having been in the presence of a deep spirit, and this somehow comforted and strengthened me. With an "Amen," he slipped into the night. *I will pray for you, George Packard,* I remember thinking as I watched him leave. *I will pray for your safety and health because we need you on this planet.*

After putting the children to bed, my husband and I discussed whether I should take the train or drive to the area. Given the late hour, I decided to drive, which I never did again until late in the spring. I remember a long embrace before I left. "Call me when you get there, okay?" my husband said. His voice was full of concern and support. "And call if you need help with directions."

"I will!" I said, walking quickly to my car. "I love you."

In those early weeks, we could only drive so far south on the FDR Drive; the usual exits for the World Trade Center area were closed. I wasn't sure how close I could get when I set out, but I knew, eventually, I would have to ditch my car for the subway.

I called my husband twice on my way downtown for help

with exits, before finding a twenty-four-hour garage on Houston—then called him again when I emerged out of the subway station at Fulton and Broadway in front of St. Paul's Chapel. I didn't call him again until 8:30 the next morning, when I was nearly home.

2

WALKING THE SITE LIKE GOD

GETTING PAST THE BARRICADES proved easier than I had thought. Bishop Packard had prepared me well. Once into the restricted area, I headed immediately to St. Paul's Episcopal Chapel to report my arrival. From there, I was instructed to walk the site, to pay attention to the workers, to offer consolation and comfort, to be a presence and a support. I was not yet assigned to the morgue. That would come in November, when the Red Cross took over the organizing and scheduling of chaplains. This first night, I was on my own to go where I felt called, and to stay alert to those in need.

I left St. Paul's and walked toward what would be referred to forever as Ground Zero. My heart was pounding a little. I wasn't sure if it was fear or adrenaline. It was a cool, clear October night. The area was crowded with fire trucks from all over the tristate area. There were police and emergency medical personnel on every corner. The ragged remains of buildings rimmed the site like battered sentries. And in the middle of it all was a smoldering pile of wreckage. The size of it was absolutely staggering. I watched as men formed a human chain, handing bucketfuls of debris down the line. *How are they ever going to clear that pile using buckets?* I wondered. Still, they worked. They worked without ceasing.

In some ways, they were the lucky ones. At least they had something to do. For many others, there was a lot of standing around and waiting; and with the waiting came the speculating. Was it still possible to find someone alive? Maybe some people were in the subway tunnels. There were all kinds of snack shops down there, weren't there? Was it true some old man had ridden a piece of the building down several stories and survived? It'd barely been three weeks since the attack. People have lived that long with almost nothing to eat, haven't they?

Talk floated on the brisk night air. As I passed by, I was usually greeted with a smile, a nod, or a friendly wave. About every ten yards, I would stop and talk to someone. Nearly everyone had a story. A fireman from a company in the Bronx told me about having been here on the eleventh. He told of the horrors of digging with his bare hands, of feeling something soft in the rocks and rubble and unearthing what turned out to be a woman's breast. Another told of discovering the intact body of a woman. As he moved toward her, her head turned. He explained how he stumbled backward, nearly jumping out of his skin. Thinking he was seeing things, he moved toward her again, and the same thing happened—her head moved. Then he realized that a steel pole had run through the back of her skull, and every time he moved forward, he stepped on the pole, causing her head to turn a little.

I listened to the stories. I memorized the faces telling them. I looked into people's eyes and invited them to give me their pain momentarily, to pour it into the bottomless bucket I was extending with my heart, to drain the images of their horror, just a little, by the telling.

I imagined myself like a funnel; I didn't accumulate or hold on to their pain—I just helped them release it. Each time a conversation seemed to reach its conclusion, I would put my hand on a shoulder or an arm, and promise to pray for the person I was talking with. And I did. I still do. I tried to lighten their burdens just a little; I tried to affirm them and support them. The collar that I had felt so ambivalent about wearing was actually an open invitation to talk. And I realized that I was grateful for it. I couldn't fathom at the time how important it was for workers to see a clergy presence at Ground Zero; but a year or so later, I read someone describe us this way: "They walked the site like God." Clearly, in times of crisis, it is essential to bear witness to the fact that we are not alone in the world. Even through the darkest valleys, we are not forsaken. And no one is forgotten.

There were also glimmers of grace on this first night, and these moments made me smile. For instance, as I made my way along a particularly desolate block, a couple of young police officers approached me anxiously. "Hey, Reverend, Reverend!" they called. "You are a reverend, aren't you?"

"Yes," I said. There was an urgency in their voices that made me think they were going to direct me to someone in need. My first impulse was that *they* were okay but were worried about someone else. I was half right—but not in the way that I had anticipated.

"Listen, we were just wondering what the difference is between a Catholic and a Protestant."

When I heard this, I felt my whole body exhale and my heart lift. No longer on red alert, I could feel the cool wind in my hair, and the evening air coloring my cheeks. I was startled and refreshed because it seemed so random and sweet a question, so ordinary and out of context in this night of sadness and despair.

"You see," said one of the officers, "my buddy here is engaged to a Protestant and he's Catholic, and they were wondering how to bring up the kids. What do you think?"

I looked at them and smiled. Their faces were so animated and full of confidence. I knew they weren't asking me for a thesis on the Protestant Reformation. They didn't want to know my thoughts on Vatican II. They were looking, in their own way, for some kind of blessing and reassurance.

"Well," I started, "there's not much difference, really, when it comes to belief. They are both Christian religions. Catholics put more emphasis on the saints, on the veneration of Mary, and on the importance of the Pope. Protestants severed their connection to Rome and pretty much did away with confession. But the main difference is in how they are organized and who gets to be ordained. Obviously, I am a prime example. I could not be a Catholic priest—and neither could you if you were married."

"Thank God for that!" they laughed. "But what do you

think we should do?" asked the young officer, eyes open wide, trusting, expectant.

"I think you should decide who is most likely to take the kids to church. To whom is religion most important—you or your fiancée? Teach the children about both traditions, but bring them up in the faith of the most actively involved parent, because it really doesn't matter to God. Just love them, love each other, and do your best."

"You sure?" asked the future groom. "Both religions believe in Jesus and God and all that stuff?"

"Yup. I'm sure. I promise."

For a moment, we stood together like a sturdy three-legged stool under the starless sky. I am sure that we were encircled in light. And the light was called hope.

"Thanks, Rev!" they said after shaking my hand. I watched them walk away, still engaged in their discussion, hands gesturing, long legs moving in easy synchronicity. A flood of gratitude washed over me as I stood there. Thank God there are those who still hope, who still plan, who still have the gumption to get engaged and to marry and to worry about raising children who are not yet born. Thank God for those who still believe in the future. "Keep them safe," I whispered, sending a prayer flying toward their backs, like a mother running with hats that her boys forgot to put on. Then they disappeared around a corner as if exiting a stage. And the night and I resumed our quiet watch.

3

SAVING ANTHONY

ABOUT 3:30 IN THE morning, I approach the corner across from what is left of Building Five. Three police officers are stationed there. They are sitting on folding chairs, looking tired, frustrated, and a little bored. "Hey, Reverend," one of them calls as I come near, "we have an officer here who is in dire need of forgiveness. He's an atheist. What do you think we should do with him?" Reaching the officer in question, I offer a mock kick to his shins, which makes them laugh. It seems to take them by surprise; it also prompts them to welcome me into their company. Another chair is somehow found and offered to me. As I gratefully accept it, I realize that this is the first time I have sat down since arriving just before midnight.

"How're you guys holding up?" I ask.

"Beautiful, just beautiful," says one of the men with a smile. It seems to be an inside joke, because they all laugh. I have the feeling they say this because there is no real way of answering that question. How *could* they be feeling, after all? What can they say, how can they put into words the effect of guarding this post? They are participants in the investigation of a crime for which there is no precedent. And so, if laughter escapes, it is heavy and tinged with melancholy.

Our conversation starts like a dance between strangers, a bit tentative and shy, until the rhythm of the stories begins to carry us. Soon the men are openly sharing their disbelief and horror over this terrible event. Though the evidence of it is right before our eyes, it is nearly impossible to take in. "I still can't believe it," confesses one of the officers, shaking his head. "I'm down here every night on this same corner, looking at the same mess, and I still can't believe it's real." Along with disbelief, there is palpable frustration. All had hoped that survivors would be pulled from the rubble. All had hoped that there would be something more for them to do than stand guard over what is feeling more and more like a graveyard. These men are trained to save lives, to stop crimes, to enforce some decent rule of law. None of them could have fathomed that one day they would be guarding the ghostly remains of part of the city they loved and nearly three thousand of her people. The night passes slowly for those whose only task is to watch and wait.

The men talk of the stress on their families. They talk of their first glimpses of violence as young cops, and of the images that never seem to leave them. They ask me about myself, about my work, and how I have come to be there with them. They listen attentively as I speak. The conversation now has an easy, gentle flow. Were it not for the grim backdrop of Ground Zero, one might mistake it for small talk. But upon closer observation, the sadness and fatigue which tug at the corners of their eyes, and the yearning they have to tell their stories, and the images they share bear witness to heartbreak and trauma. These men will never be the same.

When our conversation seems to reach its natural conclusion, this particular dance over, I decide to continue on my rounds. They smile and say to stop back if I have the chance. I get the feeling that they are reluctant to let me go. The time we spent together, however brief, has provided a welcome relief from the oppressive monotony and frustration of their shifts. To tell the truth, it is a little hard for me to move on, too, because I know that I will have to start all over again with the next person or group of people I encounter. But it is time; so I take a deep breath, say thanks for the chair, and go on my way.

For a few moments, I stand alone, looking at the pile of debris and the surrounding wreckage. I clear my mind so that I can make room for more stories, more pain. I tuck them away carefully, not to be suppressed but to be preserved. When I can feel my spirit lifting, my mind clearing, the scene around me comes into sharp focus. Perhaps the stories I have heard have released the voices and faces of the human beings buried there . . . perhaps the stories have unblocked my ears and my heart. I stand without moving, breathing slowly and deeply, as if in meditation, opening myself, and allowing the Spirit to break through.

I'm not sure how many minutes go by, but soon I become

aware of a groan emanating from the pile. It is as if someone has slowly turned up the volume from an invisible speaker. Some might say that this is my imagination. No matter. How can anyone explain a spiritual experience without sounding slightly mad? Smoke is rising into the black night air—and permeating it all is the swirling, unseen presence of the dead. I am sure that it is palpable and audible for anyone who dares to feel or to listen. My impression is that some of the dead are moaning in anguished confusion, trying to figure out what has happened to them, while others cry out because they know. I also intuit the presence of other, higher spiritual beings trying to guide them gently away from the scene of their deaths.

"Go," I whisper into the night. "Don't stay here. You are free now. This has nothing to do with you. We will look for your bodies. We will honor you. But go. Be at peace."

In the months to follow, I will experience the gradual diminishing of these groans. "Perhaps I just got used to being on-site," I will say when asked. But deep down, I will always believe that I heard them, and that eventually all who were suffering did in fact find their way home.

I begin walking again, turning my attention to the living—but the dead and I have become permanently acquainted. They walk with me as I circle the site, guiding me to those in need. They accompany me as I make my way past tattered buildings that will soon come down, past construction trucks and fire trucks, past men in hard hats and uniforms. And they will eventually give me the strength to see their broken bodies and to offer blessing.

For an hour or two, I weave a path among the countless

men and women who are working, perhaps unknowingly, in the company of the dead. Immersed in thought, I am startled to find myself passing the same corner occupied by the officers who had offered me the chair. They wave me over like they have something important to discuss, something they have been thinking about since I left them.

"Hey, guys, what's up?" I ask.

The captain tells me about an officer in his precinct. At first, I think he is just teasing me, having a little fun at my expense—but the more he talks, the more genuine seems his concern.

"I've got this guy, Anthony," he begins. "And believe you me, Reverend, he needs saving. This guy is such a bad apple. He cheats on his wife, he runs around constantly with other women . . . It's bad for morale at the station. I mean, we can't take it anymore. You've got to save him, Rev, put the fear of God back into him."

I look at the captain, studying his face, and then at the other two officers. This wasn't at all what I had expected, but it seems to be what God is presenting me with. "What do you suggest?" I ask. "Do you want me to offer him some sort of opportunity for confession? Do you want me to help you confront him? Or do you just want me to tell him that God has told me everything he's been doing and he'd better stop?"

I am joking about the latter, of course, but the captain and his companions begin to hatch a plan to save their fellow officer. I am fully aware that this is born most likely out of a desire to break the unbearable heaviness and monotony of their night, and to distract them, even momentarily, from the senseless destruction in which they are entrenched. I wonder again how concerned they actually are for Anthony's soul.

"This is what you do," says the captain with a twinkle in his eye. "See that guy on the corner? That's Anthony's partner. Ask for Anthony. Say he helped you out once and you want to say thank you."

"Where's Anthony?" I ask, beginning to get a queasy feeling in my stomach.

"He's asleep in the police van there."

"Wait a minute! You want me to wake up an officer who's been working all night just to pull a prank on him?"

"First of all, he's been sleeping too long. Second of all, Rev, this is not a prank. It's for his own good, remember? This is for his soul and for the morale of the precinct. He won't know if you're someone he met at a bar or what—and I guarantee he'll start hitting on you."

"Come on, guys, I'm too old for this," I argue, suddenly feeling a little ridiculous and wishing I were still the twenty-six-year-old I was when I was first ordained.

"Please, Reverend. Please do this for us," they plead. "We've been down here every night since this thing happened, and, trust us, there are not too many opportunities for a little levity. Besides, his behavior really is detrimental to the other guys in the precinct."

I look into the blue, bloodshot eyes of the captain and then to his fellow officers; I look from one to the other to the other. Sighing, I put my head in my hands and reluctantly say, "Okay. Okay. I will do this for you. I will do this for Anthony and for you, his comrades." *Is this professional?* I ask myself. *Is it appropriate? Is it disrespectful? Would the bishop approve?* I don't have time to ponder these questions; the wheels have already started moving. I take a deep breath and head with long, determined strides for the corner where Anthony's partner is sitting. Instinctively, I pull out the white tab from my clergy collar and tuck it into my pocket. I give my hair a shake and square my shoulders. "God, forgive me," I mutter, glancing up at the not yet dawning sky.

As I near the corner, I glance over my shoulder and can see the creeping shadows of the officers, who have followed me. They are hiding behind trailers and vans to get a good view of their wayward colleague about to be busted by the female priest. It is too late to turn back, so I ignore my ambivalence and my reservations, and ask for Anthony. His partner jumps up a little too quickly, like he's accustomed to strange women asking for his friend. Despite my fake protests, the partner says he'll go and wake Anthony from the trailer.

After a minute or two, Anthony emerges, sleepy-eyed but smoothing his hair. No, he's not sure he remembers me. How long has it been? I bluff. I smile. I say it's okay if he doesn't remember. Meanwhile, I can see that the half-hidden officers are enjoying this. They are beginning to stifle silent laughter in the shadows; I can see their shoulders shaking. As if on cue, Anthony begins to work his charm. When do I finish my shift? Will I be coming down regularly to help out? True to his reputation, but obviously not to his wedding vows, Officer Anthony makes his move: Do I have a number where he can reach me?

No longer able to contain themselves, the captain and his

fellow officers jump out of hiding and begin to verbally accost him.

"Anthony, do you know who this is? This is a priest you're trying to pick up! That's practically like hitting on God! You're going straight to hell, Anthony. Do you hear me?" says the captain with a triumphant laugh. *"Straight . . . to . . . hell!"*

Anthony tries to protest as he looks at me in disbelief. He says he wasn't really trying to hit on me, but no one is buying it. With each denial, the other officers get more animated. Not to be outdone, Anthony turns to me and says with a smile, "So, what time *do* you get off?" The officers laugh, as we turn to walk away. But their laughter dies quickly, like a match in the wind, as we head toward our posts.

"Thanks, Rev," the captain says softly as heaviness begins to creep into his eyes again. "You really made our night. Thanks a lot for being here. For all of us."

"I'll keep Anthony in my prayers," I say, shaking his hand. "And you, too. Be careful, okay?"

"Hey, we're always careful, right, fellas?"

"Sure," one of them answers. "Beautiful."

4

THE MORGUE CALLS

AS MORNING DAWNED, MY shift came to an end. I
watched the sky change from purple to pink to blue, wa-
tercolors running and seeping across a giant canvas. Workers
were steadily coming and going, the ready replacing the weary.
They nodded to one another, they shook hands, they filled one
another's shoes. The site, too, seemed to shift and change. The
ghosts were quiet. Maybe they were observing us, maybe they
were sleeping; or maybe they were just drowned out by the
bustle of a new day, camouflaged by the light. I went into St.
Paul's to say good-bye and to let the priest in charge know that
I was leaving. Then I boarded the subway, got off several blocks
uptown, found my car, and started the drive home.

The FDR was humming with morning commuters. Luck-
ily for me, most of them were heading south. The northbound
side, on which I was traveling, was smooth and fast. Cars wove
in and out of the lanes like sewing needles stitching a pattern.

As for me, I just drove. I could not process. I could not think profound thoughts or even, momentarily, recall some of my conversations. Each mile brought me closer to my life, closer to the ordinary realities that filled my days—my family, my job, the responsibilities of living. And yet something had shifted in me. It was imperceptible, really—but I knew that I had made a heart commitment to the workers and the victims at Ground Zero.

I arrived home just in time to kiss my children as they left for school. "Are you okay, Mommy?" my daughter asked, wide-eyed. "I'm so glad you're home."

"I'm fine, honey," I said as I gave her an extralong squeeze. "I'm fine."

I rested for two hours before heading to my job at hospice. There were patients to see, families to help. Death loomed like a shadow. I could not help but make the comparison between having the opportunity to prepare for death and dying suddenly, between gently assisting a family through the dying process and looking for the shattered remains of loved ones who just never came home from work. Grief is grief, as some would say, but it does matter how one dies and how remains are handled. It matters to those who are still here, those who must come to terms with living without a loved one.

I completed my day vaguely aware of the lack of support I felt from my colleagues. Most knew why I was late to work, yet only one or two people asked me how I was. I observed their silence as if from a distance. The concern was not that I had stayed up all night helping those working downtown but whether I could be present to our patients. I admired their commitment to maintaining excellent care, and the unspoken reminder that these patients were important, but I found it disheartening that so few coworkers could find it in themselves to ask, "How ya doin'?"

This continued to be the case throughout my months of service downtown. There were exceptions, but I still find it curious and infuriating when I reflect back on that time. My commitment to hospice never wavered, nor did I ever underestimate the pain of these families; but, for a time, I had to stretch. Sometimes I was tired. Sometimes, I'm sure, I was numb. But always I tried to give the best I had, aware that this acute crisis in our nation's history would pass, even if its impact on me would remain.

A few weeks went by. Then, on November 13, 2001, I found myself in a room at the offices of the Episcopal Diocese of New York with about fifty other ministers, priests, and rabbis. The Rev. Tom Faulkner, an Episcopal priest, had called us together on behalf of the Red Cross, who were now officially taking over the organizing of chaplains at Ground Zero. No one was sure what this change of leadership would mean, but Tom assured everyone that it would help smooth our efforts.

The atmosphere was both determined and anxious. It was the day after Flight 587 had crashed in Queens. The plane had been headed to Santo Domingo in the Dominican Republic but fell from the sky shortly after takeoff, killing all 260 people onboard and 5 on the ground. Though terrorism was ruled out fairly quickly, it was obviously on all of our minds. An announcement was made that there was still a need for clergy at the airport, where families were gathering, as well as at the crash site to offer blessings over the dead and support to the workers. Anyone who was able to volunteer for this effort was directed to gather immediately after our meeting.

I considered whether it would be possible for me to volunteer. The impulse to offer my services was tempered by the reality that I needed coverage for my children. This would be a frequent dilemma for me as I volunteered at Ground Zero: how to balance my call to service with my commitment to family. I envied those whose children were grown, or who had no family responsibilities. As much as I felt I could be helpful, I knew that this time I would have to pass.

During the meeting, the various opportunities for ministry at Ground Zero were outlined. There would be several family centers, St. Paul's Chapel, the Marriott Hotel (where meals were currently being offered to workers), the Permanent Morgue, which was off-site, and the Temporary Morgue located at Ground Zero. I knew, without hesitation, that my call was to the Temporary Morgue, or the T-Mort, as it came to be known. I felt that my experience with the dying and the dead had prepared me as well as it could for being on hand to offer blessings over remains and comfort to the bereaved. I could not truly fathom what awaited me, or any of us, at the T-Mort. We were simply moving with whatever current was carrying us to our places of service. For me, volunteering at the morgue was the only choice. In a strange way, I knew that I would be most at home there—at home with the dead and with the people who were working so hard to honor them.

Ministry at the morgue did not entail therapy, and it did not involve religious service in a traditional way. As the days unfolded, our mission became clear. We were to offer a quiet ministry of presence at a time of utter despair. We were to walk with the weary and the broken, to offer blessings over the remains of colleagues and strangers, to lift the human spirit if possible, and to bear witness to the enduring Beauty of life. Anyone who served at Ground Zero, who walked with fellow workers through that valley of the shadow of death, encountered terrible destruction and unbearable sorrow. But what we left with, miraculously, was a pearl of great price: the awareness of the Holy, living and vibrant, in the eyes of other human beings.

5

MIST AND VAPOR

Y OU MIGHT WANT A little of this," says the cop standing
next to me, holding a jar of mentholated vapor rub. He
swipes some around his nostrils, getting a little in his mustache,
and offers some to me. As I meet his eyes, he says, "It doesn't
help much, but it's something. This one's gonna be bad." I hesi-
tate but do as he suggests, rubbing the base of my nose with the
ointment. The menthol clears my sinuses with its cool, sharp
vapor. It reminds me of being a child, when my mother would
rub my chest with Vicks. I remember her silhouette appearing
against the light in the hall as she entered my dark, little room.
The sweetness of her voice and her gentle touch almost made
it worth being sick. I would surrender to the sound of her, the
feel of her, trusting implicitly in her care for me. As she disappeared back into the light, I would snuggle down into the soft
darkness of my room, breathe in the familiar vapor, and know
that everything would be better in the morning.

But now I am standing in the harsh glare of a fluorescent light. And what emerges from the doorway beyond our trailer is not my mother with her healing touch but a large black body bag. Everything has been turned inside out. The darkness is not cozy—it is terrifying. It holds the gruesome reality of our worst nightmares. It lurks behind curtains of concrete and mud, steel and shattered glass. And the light? The light, too, has lost its comfort. It is no longer where mothers appear and disappear to keep the world in order; it is where we are forced to bear witness time and again to the unthinkable.

The body bag is placed on one of the receiving tables. It is obvious that it contains a sizable human remain. I feel my chest tighten and my breath constrict. *Oh, dear God,* I say to myself, *please help me.* But nothing can prepare us for this ritual. No matter how many bags are brought in, no matter how many bodies or fragments of bodies we see, the shock of opening that bag is always the same. Dear God dear God dear God. How many times can the heart be broken? *Just once more,* you always think to yourself. *I can do it one more time. We can do it. Steady now. Pass me the Vicks, brother. Pass me the Vicks.*

We assemble, as always, in silence. The bag is unzipped. Holy God. There is the torso of a man in what looks to have been a white, button-down shirt. There is no head. There is nothing beyond the tops of the hips. The shirt is shredded and muddy. The rib cage exposed. There are no arms or hands. God have mercy. The Vicks doesn't really help. This one has been imprisoned for too long below the rubble. Decay is in my mouth. It is in my throat. It is in my soul now, too. As I inhale, the dead lodge themselves within me. I will carry them around in my body, in my gut, in my mucous membranes, and in my cells. This one is stuck in my chest. *Someone's father,* I keep thinking. *Someone's son.* We go about our work like phantoms, like holograms of ourselves. No one looks away. We cannot look away. *Bear witness,* this torso of a man whispers. *This happened. I died. Live anyway. Keep breathing.*

The blessing is the last thing that happens before the bag is zipped closed. I am aware that my words will fall like mist, like dew, like an anointing or baptism. I will rub this chest with the vapor of my breath, with words, because that is all I have. Will they soothe? Will they comfort? Will they be enough?

Without knowing it, we form a circle of light around the man—but it is not the harsh glare of fluorescent light. It is the warm glow from the hallway, from childhoods where life made sense, and mothers came when you were afraid, and darkness was only a blanket you snuggled into on your way to a delicious dream. We do the best we can in our too bright trailer. With our presence and our words and our broken hearts, we rock this man on his makeshift bed, tuck him in, then send him gently on his way toward home. *Now perhaps he can rest,* I think. But for those of us who remain, it is more complicated. We stand, dumbfounded, blinking in the light, like those waving from a train platform. He is gone, but we are here, waiting for the darkness to surrender, once again, that which it has stolen.

6

ADAM'S HAND

It is a rainy November afternoon at the site. I have been in the morgue for a couple of hours talking to the EMTs and cops, but it has been quiet in terms of remains. All of us hope the phone will ring or a radio will announce a new discovery. In the meantime, we make ourselves busy. We talk, we stretch; we stare at the ceiling. We decide to get a bite at St. Paul's or the Marriott or the Salvation Army Respite Center, fondly referred to as the big bubble. I am free to walk the site, to stop and talk to workers, and to pause for a while with those who need to tell their stories.

I step out into the drizzle, put my head down, and walk to the corner closest to where the south tower stood. The world is monochromatic; everything melts together in a watery gray—the sky, the muddy ground, the buildings. Trucks and machinery drone on without ceasing, providing a perfect sound track for the dreariness of the day. The air smells of diesel and muck and who knows what else. It has a bitter and peculiar taste, and burns my eyes and throat. It crosses my mind that we are all swimming in a toxic cesspool, but what can we do?

"It's bad down here today," says a police officer on the corner without much expression. I nod in agreement and shudder a little. As we begin to make small talk, I notice the familiar resignation that has wrapped itself around him. I have the feeling that he, like so many others, has been here too often, has seen too much, and that no amount of rest can ease his weariness now. It has settled in his bones, in his identity. We slip into an easy exchange about everyday life. The officer is in his early forties. "If I could retire tomorrow, I would," he tells me. "I could practically retire now, but it just doesn't seem like the right time to leave. It would feel unpatriotic, you know? I couldn't leave now." We talk of his children. Yes, they are proud of him. Yes, they worry. Yes, there is a strain on his marriage with all the time he is putting in at the Trade Center.

"I've gone to too many funerals and memorials," he tells me. "At the last one I went to, a twelve-year-old girl gave the eulogy for her dad. She was the same age as my daughter. All I could think of was that no kid should have to do that. No kid should lose her father this way. Right then and there, I decided to get out when I can so that my daughters won't have to do that for me."

"You're a young man," I say. "What kind of work do you think you will do after you leave the police force?"

"I don't know, but it'll have nothing to do with law enforcement. Maybe something like landscaping. Be outside. Make something grow."

I put my hand on his arm for a moment and look into his face. There is still something alive there—a shimmer of color amidst all this grayness, like a green shoot pushing its way through a crack in the cement.

"Do that," I say to him. "In the meantime, teach your girls."

"Thanks," he says, with a faint smile. "Take care."

With that he dismisses me. One can only talk so much here. I understand, and I keep moving.

November becomes December, and the days begin to blur. I now have trouble remembering what I did on a particular shift. With whom did I talk? What part of someone did I bless? Between volunteering at the morgue, working at hospice, and taking care of my children, I am beginning to forget—or am I storing the memories away in some locked vault of me? I feel as shattered as the skull fragment before me. It is night again, and I find myself looking blankly at the smooth bone which the medical examiner turns over in his hand like a small stone. I imagine that he is going to skip it across some placid lake, like I used to do with rocks when I was young. I no longer bother with the mentholated ointment. I know too well that nothing can blot out the reality of death that permeates our lives here.

Once identified, the skull fragment is gently set aside. There is tissue. There are random, unidentifiable bone chips. Then the medical examiner carefully extracts what turns out to be a left hand from the bag on the table. Someone lets out a soft, anguished groan. The sound escapes not because of the grimness of the discovery but because of what hangs precariously on the tip of one finger—a wedding ring. It is a miracle which we all recognize immediately. How they managed to extract this hand from that hellish mess with the ring still there seems impossible. The ring circles the last knuckle of the ring finger, which is curled ever so slightly toward the palm—just enough to have kept its treasure. Kept its promise. The hand is blackened and somewhat atrophied. And yet it is beautiful. A man's hand bearing witness to love. A man's hand bearing witness to the excruciating care of those who unearthed it. A man's hand which was once a boy's, which was formed in his mother's womb, which first was feather soft as it curled in a tiny fist, which grew to hold a ball, to roll a truck, to move a pencil, to write a name. This hand waved hello to friends; it tied shoes and buttoned shirts. This hand tenderly caressed a spouse; it was offered to another in love as a life together began. Did it also hold a child's hand? Did it rock a cradle, hold a bottle? Did it fix a broken toy? Someone will get their husband's ring back, we whisper. Unbelievable.

It rests before us now, as if plucked from the ceiling of the Sistine Chapel. As such, it is more than the hand of this particular man—it is the hand of a saint. It is Michelangelo's Adam reaching for God, or God reaching for us. It is the charred evidence of when life leapt like a spark from the Divine. We cannot speak. This hand reaches for us in all its aching beauty as if to say, "Behold. Behold the utter stupidity and brutality of the human race. Behold its stubborn grace. I made you. I reached for you, and once you knew enough to reach for me. I encircled you in love. I cling to you still, like this golden circle. Reach for me again, and live."

Two years later, I will dream that I am carrying this hand, now restored to a healthy, fleshy pink. It is my job to find to whom it belongs. I am walking quickly down unfamiliar streets, looking, looking, looking for the owner. I know that he is here somewhere. I am sorry that it has taken me so long. I am determined but bewildered. I continue searching as I cradle it in my own two hands. "Where are you? Where are you?" I call.

But before this night is even thinking about becoming a dream, I return home exhausted, drop my clothes on the floor, and curl into bed. It is nearly 2:00 AM. "Are you okay?" my husband asks sleepily. "They found a hand with a wedding ring," I whisper. And then I begin to cry.

7

FLAGS AND TAGS

Another Saturday night at the morgue. A body bag lies on one of the stainless steel tables. It is not one of the small red bundles that are often lying there, usually containing but a fragment of human remains. This one contains the nearly intact body of a construction worker. A teamster, I'm told. The blessing has already been given by the chaplain preceding me. I just missed him. Subway seemed to take forever from Grand Central tonight.

I check in at the Temporary Morgue, introducing myself to the captain in charge and leaving my cell phone number on the wall. Then I meet my husband and two children on the sidewalk in the nonrestricted area. For the first time since I began volunteering at the morgue, they have ridden the train down with me. I wanted them to get a glimpse of where I go. Take some of the anxiety out of it for the children. As we begin the walk down to St. Paul's, they seem to respond to the pulse of life in the cold January air. The sidewalks are crowded with people. The night smells of pretzels and roasted nuts, of hot dogs and, occasionally, wet concrete. As we approach St. Paul's, I see that there is a long line of people waiting to walk out onto the new viewing platform. They need to see, we all need to see; it is our communal tragedy. But I know that, no matter how long they look, it will never make sense. The only thing that makes sense is their presence. Someone needs to bear witness to what is happening here every hour, every minute of every long day and lonely night.

We duck into the church. It envelops us in its hushed peace, offering a welcome contrast to the bustle outside. A violin and a piano play a soft, haunting tune. Cops and firemen are scattered throughout the pews. Some sit alone, staring straight ahead; some talk quietly to one another. Food and coffee are offered and gratefully accepted. There is an awkward line for a bathroom that was never intended to accommodate such a volume of patrons. A young man in uniform appears almost unconscious as he stretches out on a massage therapist's table. I envy her ability to offer something of concrete comfort to these men and women. By now, I am well acquainted with their stories of standing for hours in the bitter cold. *Rest,* I think to myself, looking at him. *Rest and surrender to a moment of peace.*

I sit with my family for a while in one of the pews. There are pillows scattered throughout the benches. The church walls are covered with notes, banners, cards, and pictures from all over the world. They offer support, encouragement, gratitude, and comfort. *Holy graffiti,* I think to myself. *Holy graffiti.*

Soon I feel the morgue tugging at me. My phone hasn't rung, but I feel anxious to get going. We emerge from the church and head back toward the Temporary Morgue. I say good-bye to my husband and children on the street. My daughter keeps turning around to wave. Her face is filled with a mixture of awe and anxiety. *What is she thinking?* I wonder. *What can she comprehend? What fears and images creep into her eight-year-old head?* My son skips beside my husband, eyes drinking in all the men in uniform. Living G.I. Joes. He is spared the enormity of the event because he is six years old and life is still magical and sane.

I open the door to the morgue and see a couple of EMTs I've met here before. I'm amazed at how good it is to see a familiar face, to feel a sense of continuity, to skip the introductions and the work it takes to establish a rapport. Most of my contacts here, most of those with whom I have had conversations, I never see again. We meet, I hear their stories, our hearts connect, then—gone. Their faces will fade before their stories, I suppose.

It soon gets busy. A couple of bags of remains are brought in. At this point, the magic number is three. When three bags are brought in, the medical examiner and crime scene investigator will be called, and the procedure in the morgue will begin. This procedure differs only if a full body or the remains of a man or woman of service is brought in. Then there is no waiting.

Two bundles in red plastic bags sit on the receiving table. A TV is perched precariously on top of a tall, metal shelf. CNN is broadcasting the news of a small plane that has crashed into a building in Tampa. I feel numb as I watch the story unfold. A weary-looking EMT says, to no one in particular, "I bet it was a suicide. That's just my feeling. Feels like a suicide." The next day, I hear on the news that he is right. The fifteen-year-old student pilot left a note saying that he endorsed the terrorism of September 11. But tonight, we can only speculate (if we have the interest or the energy to do so). Conversation drifts. Workers come and go. There is a shift change. Badges and radios and keys are exchanged.

The EMS lieutenant in charge begins to tell me of his youngest daughter, who has a history of running away from home. She suffers from bipolar disorder, he says. Out of the blue, he informs me that he oscillates between being a heathen and being an agnostic. I'm not sure how he would define these, but it doesn't matter. "I believe in God," he says, "but who's to say that Islam is not the way?" I smile, knowing that he is not looking for an answer—he is nudging me, sticking his toe into the water to see how I will react. I ask him more about his family. He takes a Christmas cookie out of a box next to him and pops it into his mouth. "Look at me," he says. "Eating cookies in the morgue. Pretty gross, eh?" "That's what they're there for," I answer. But I, too, am aware of the remains on the table next to me. Whenever someone walks past, the smell of decay catches in my throat.

How strangely comfortable we have become with the bits of humanity waiting patiently in their bags. Patience has become a necessary part of survival here. To watch the pieces of people being extracted from that pit is to watch something of extraordinary patience and commitment. Much of the work is done by hand. When it was clear that no life would be pulled from the wreckage, the meticulous collecting of remains began. It is holy work. And what is most miraculous of all is the fact that everyone senses this. When conversation goes on in the morgue, with people seemingly oblivious to the fact that there is some bit of someone sitting in that bag, it can be deceiving. No one has forgotten, not even for an instant. No one is unaware. No one is callous. They have only accepted, out of necessity, the pace of this process. For everyone here knows, when the bags are opened, they will not look away. There will be reverence and respect. A hush will fill the room. The medical examiner will gently and attentively struggle to make out what bit of the body is before him. The crime scene investigator will photograph the remains and document where the victim was found. An entry will be made into the log. A chaplain will offer a blessing. Grown men and women will cross themselves and bow their heads. And then it will be back to waiting and hoping that more remains will be recovered during the night, plucked from the dust and the anonymity of this communal grave.

Midway through the evening, one of the EMTs says that he is in need of more flags with which to drape the remains of the dead. Flags had originally been reserved for people of service but now are draped over any substantial body that is recovered. It is the right thing to do; for all who died were inadvertently drafted into service—for their country, for their coworkers, for the rest of us who remain, the walking wounded. The EMT tells us that some flags have been stolen off his gator as he's driven through the streets. "Someone wanted to trade me a picture of the Trade Center for a flag," he says, shaking his head. There is not much response from the others in the morgue. A few people shrug and look idly away. The lieutenant says that he will get more flags right away.

About 11:00 PM, the lieutenant returns with two boxes of flags. As he lifts a box up to the top of a shelf, I can't help noticing that it goes right next to a box labeled TOE TAGS. *Flags and tags,* I say to myself. *This is what it has come down to, flags and tags.* The only problem is there are too few toes to tag. Most still lie hidden somewhere beneath the rubble or have been blown out to sea on the fall breeze, now turned cold. If we could find the dead, we would honor them. But for now, we can only be patient and wait.

8

STATION 10–10

IT IS GETTING CLOSE to midnight. I have had too much
coffee, too many bottles of water, and have made too many
trips to St. Paul's to use the bathroom. I decide to walk down
to the fire station that sits on the edge of Ground Zero. Once
nestled in the shadow of the mighty towers, it is a place that
some workers avoid and others seek out like a holy shrine. The
firefighters from this company were the first to respond when
the planes hit. "All rushed in to help," I hear over and over. "No
one came out." Someone tells me that all of the men from this
station were killed on that morning because they were in the
middle of a shift change. As the months pass, I learn that five
men from Station 10–10 were killed that day—five more than
anyone can bear—but not *all* of the men from this company.
Truth and mythology mingle freely in the air in these early days
of the recovery, adding to the haunting sense of tragedy and
shock. For the moment, for those who walk the site, however,

facts are less important than feelings, numbers less compelling than the battered station that still stands defiantly at its post.

Now the firehouse is ghostly quiet, save for a few scattered workers. Supplies have been organized in the bay that once housed a fire truck. Someone is on hand to give out gloves, hats, boots, socks, et cetera to the workers. As the hours pass, the man on duty sits at a makeshift desk talking quietly to those who come in and out. There are a variety of fire department patches scattered across the desk, free to whoever wants one. Another man sits behind a computer in a small office. He is in charge of satellite locating—when remains are found, he precisely charts the place, the position, and the time.

I offer the usual "How ya doin'?" to those men I pass. There *are* women here, but it is predominately a man's world at Ground Zero. When I worked my first shift, back in October, the air was positively humming with male energy, with testosterone, and with what could have been mistaken for bravado. But it was not bravado; it was the desperation of strong and able men who could not fathom that there was nothing they could do to save a life. They lined their trucks along the site, made plans, climbed the pile, passed buckets of debris like thimblefuls of ocean. They persisted with their broad shoulders and bare hands, with images of their children at home and their brothers underground, and they hoped.

Now, some four months later, they work continuously to find the bodies of those who eluded their best intentions to save. It requires tremendous strength and gut-wrenching commitment. But what always makes my throat tighten and my eyes well is the quiet tenderness with which they go about their work. "See how the driver of that bulldozer gives his bucket a little shake?" says a man standing next to me. "You know why he does that? He does that to make sure he doesn't have a piece of someone caught in his bucket. He's trying to see if anything can be shaken loose from the rubble so that no remains are lost." These men no longer hope for the rescue of victims, or even for whole bodies. Perhaps the only thing they hope is that no one will get hurt this night, or that sleep will come quickly when they finally go home.

As I step into Station 10–10, I give a small wave to the man tending the supplies and walk quietly into what was the dining room for those who belonged to this firehouse. It is as if the room has been frozen in time. No one uses this space out of respect for the men who died. Notes of upcoming events, long since past, hang on a wall. There are a few boxes of pancake mix and pasta on the counter. Pictures and plaques keep watch from their places as if standing guard. There is a feeling of warmth and familiarity, of comfort and casual ease. *They are never coming back,* I think. *They are never going to sit around this table and laugh at someone's stupid joke or argue over the Yankees and the Mets, the Jets and the Giants. No one will announce his engagement or the birth of a new baby.* "God bless you all," I whisper to no one—or to everyone.

I walk down the hall to use the bathroom. After shutting and locking the outside door, I am certain that I hear someone using the urinal next to my stall. My heart jumps. I look under the door but see no feet. With blood beginning to pump in my ears, I quickly finish and open the stall door. I notice that the water in the sink is running. *Was it running when I came in?* I wonder. Then I hear something behind me that sounds very much like someone ripping a paper towel out of the dispenser. No one there. My heart is now pounding. I open the door to the bathroom and nearly trip over a fireman who is on his hands and knees pulling duct tape off the carpet just outside the door. "Sorry," I say awkwardly, turning red. He looks up and smiles. His eyes are kind, his voice genuinely warm. "That's okay. Be careful now."

I feel a little ridiculous as I walk back through the doors into the night, but a lingering feeling of the unseen presence of those who died remains. A band of men who loved this house, who laughed and slept here, and did their jobs, are dead. *Are you here now?* I ask silently, looking up into the black night sky. *Are your bodies still out there? Are you okay? Are you trying to help?*

The slap of bitter cold January air interrupts my communion with the dead, and I walk with long, quick strides toward the morgue. I check my cell phone on the way. No calls. I feel as if I have been gone for hours, but it has been more like thirty minutes. Once inside the morgue trailer, which could never be described as cozy, I am comforted by the reality of live workers, with real voices and jobs to be done. As I slip into one of the folding chairs that line the wall, a female EMT asks me where I've been. "I went down to 10–10 to use the bathroom," I say.

"I never go down there," she says, flinching. "It's just too creepy."

9

THE MEDICAL EXAMINER

I will praise thee; for I am fearfully and wonderfully made.
—PSALM 139:14

THE MEDICAL EXAMINER IS a large man with a round, pleasant face. Dressed in a white, short-sleeved shirt, he will be with us for the night in the morgue, examining body parts as they are brought in, identifying them, and placing them like shattered puzzle pieces on one of the bare stainless steel tables. As I look at him, I realize that I am taking him in, holding him up like a curiosity in the light, turning him this way and that—much like he will be studying the bones and flesh that are destined to appear before us. He will try to place these fragments in the context of the human body, while I try to place him in the context of the human psyche. *Who could do his work?* I wonder. *Who could examine dead bodies, day after day, trying to determine cause of death, time of death?* I look, vaguely, for signs of oddity in his presence, but he seems more like a friendly visitor from Minnesota than a seasoned medical examiner from New York City.

When I report to the Temporary Morgue for my shift, I'm told the medical examiner is sleeping. It has been a quiet evening. This is difficult for many reasons. It is April, and the recovery process is slowing dramatically. With it, a growing determination to find something, anything, of human remains hangs heavily in the air. When hours go by and not a shred of a body is found, spirits sag and the night hours crawl. Like the endless drip of a leaky faucet, time moves—slowly—but each dripping second frays the nerves. The pressure builds, and then . . . nothing. Nothing. Just the hum of machines and the silent dance of men raking, raking the dust without ceasing, looking for what feels like a needle in a smoldering haystack. Only it is not a needle buried in the dust but the splintered bodies of brothers and sisters, mothers and fathers, sons and daughters.

After several quiet hours, a few small bags of remains and a lone fireman's boot are brought into the narrow trailer. As they are placed gently on one of the two receiving tables, the room begins to come alive. Someone flips on the fluorescent light; we blink for a moment, adjusting to the sudden brightness and the activity. It is 3:30 in the morning. Tired workers get up from the hard folding chairs on which they have been dozing and stretch. An EMT goes to wake the medical examiner, who is sleeping in an adjacent trailer. After a few minutes, he appears, walking heavily into the small space without a word. Now everything snaps into sharp focus. We take our places and begin what has become a familiar routine. I feel myself take a deep breath. The crime scene investigator is ready to photograph what has been recovered—evidence of the crime which took place some seven months ago—and an EMT stands by with the log in which each recovery is recorded by hand. I am there, too, to offer what little blessing I can over these broken bits of humanity.

We watch in silence as the medical examiner begins with the boot. He takes it carefully in his large hands, and what he does next makes me suck an involuntary breath between my teeth. He puts the boot to his nose and matter-of-factly sniffs. Then he sniffs it again. "No," he says without expression. "No remains in here." "Are you sure?" someone asks. "I'd be able to smell decay," he answers. He puts the boot gently aside, and I see him give a small, respectful nod to the fireman standing by. As their eyes meet, I notice that the medical examiner is not without emotion, he is bone weary. Literally. Without a word he moves on to one of the small red plastic bags. Again the room is silent, motionless. He extracts from the bag what looks to be a four-inch piece of muddy cloth—only it is not cloth, it is tissue. "Human tissue," he says purposefully. "Site unspecified." The crime scene investigator steps up to the table to photograph the remains; it is recorded in the log with the date, time, and description. I understand that my blessing will have to wait until all the bags are opened. This has become the custom in these last days of the recovery process.

The medical examiner moves on to the next bag. Like a magician preparing to pull a rabbit from a hat, he carefully opens the bag while we wait to see what he will extract. Voilà. This time it is a perfect piece of rib, impossibly elegant, delicately curved and pure white, as if it had been meticulously scrubbed. It is about eight inches long. "Human rib," the M.E. announces without looking up, but I notice that his voice has softened ever so slightly, as have his features. Pausing, he holds the bone gently in his thick fingers, bringing it up to eye level. His expression is one of utter appreciation and reverence, like that of someone who is seeing a familiar but magnificent piece of art up close for the first time. "Look at this," he says to no one in particular. "It is brilliantly constructed. See the curve right here? See how it is bent inward just a little? This not only holds the muscles in place but it also protects the organs. It is pure genius."

I don't know if he is a religious man, but the room has become a sanctuary. I watch him in wonder. The contrast between his fleshy fingers and the graceful arc of the naked rib is almost too much to bear. Does he see that there is light streaming from what he holds in his hand? Does anyone else see this? His face is enraptured, like a child's. I am struck by his reverence but I also have the impulse to snatch the rib from him, to run from the trailer with the bone in my hand, screaming, "Here it is! Here it is! Whoever you are, I have your rib!" I want desperately to put it back in the body from which it came. It feels terribly wrong to have this piece of humanity, exposed and broken before us in this way. Something so private should not be viewed under the harsh glare of a fluorescent light, no matter how respectfully it is handled. For some reason, I feel ashamed; and I keep thinking that someone must have reached inside somebody else, dug his fingers into another's side, and extracted this something that didn't belong to him. I picture this body whole, perfect, but with a shaft of brilliant light pouring from the wound. *Put it back,* I keep repeating to myself. Trouble is, there is nowhere to put it. There is no body waiting for it, save the one I see in my mind, floating, forgiving, patient. Still, I want the medical examiner, with all his knowledge and appreciation, with his gentle, chubby fingers and his artist's eye, to find a way to return it to its rightful owner.

We are fearfully and wonderfully made, I hear in my head, and I am filled with awe. But, more than that, I am painfully aware that this perfect rib belonged to Someone. A specific Someone with a specific life and history and future that did not include dying on September 11. This rib is not art. It is not science. It is not a relic. It is evidence of a life that is no more. It bears the echo of sorrow and the DNA of generations past. It is a life that will not be repeated, replicated, replaced.

I look up just as the medical examiner gives me a nod. His work for the moment is done, while mine is just beginning. I look around the room and indicate, softly, that it is now time to offer a blessing on the remains. As always, the six or seven men and women who are gathered there, shoulder to shoulder, remove their hats and bow their heads. It is an act that always moves me. Contrary to what one may think, after so many months, it never feels routine or obligatory, just as the silence in the room never feels impatient or merely tolerant. It is filled with an intuitive awareness of Something Greater than ourselves. In this act of blessing remains, we are remembering something essential about being human, namely that life matters. It matters how we live and how we die, and how we are treated when we are dead. It means that *we* matter and, more important, that someone will remember that we matter. Honoring the dead is an inherently stubborn affirmation of life. And when you are surrounded by death, this may be the only lifeline available.

"Dear Lord," I begin. "You alone know to whom these parts belong. You knit the tissue before us, perfectly integrating it into the body. You placed this rib just so to give structure and form to one that once knew life. You know the foot that wore this boot that walked into hell for the sake of another human being and emerged into paradise. We commend these persons to your care. Receive them into the arms of your mercy, comfort the families who mourn them, and bless those who toil night and day so that others might be granted some small measure of peace. In your holy name we pray. Amen."

With that, hats are returned to heads, feet begin to shuffle out of the morgue into the night, and the stars, while invisible and silent, bear witness.

10

MAY 6, 2002

IT IS JUST BEFORE midnight when I arrive on-site. I pull my car into the small lot in front of the morgue. The roads are open to the public now, which makes driving easier, at least for these late-night shifts. The priest I am relieving looks tired. Our eyes meet, but only briefly. I recognize in him that familiar feeling of being glad the next chaplain has arrived, yet finding it difficult to leave. Where to go from here? Where do we ever go from here? We exchange few words. He tells me that it has been a quiet night, says his good-byes, then disappears into the city beyond the site.

I introduce myself to the two EMTs who are sitting side by side at a long folding table with their heads down. They smile sleepily but obviously don't feel like talking. Talking has dwindled, along with the recovery of remains. Even the desire to connect, to form some sort of bond, seems to have faded. I flip through the book in which the remains are logged. It is clear from the entries that the recovery efforts are yielding very little now—a bone fragment, a piece of tissue . . . It crosses my mind that it is going to be a very long, quiet night.

I step outside and survey the site. The cool air reminds me of the first night I spent here, in early October; but what I see is very different. Instead of the seemingly insurmountable pile, smoldering against a backdrop of shattered buildings, there is an increasingly neat pit. For a while, I watch the firemen raking through the dirt. They are moving meticulously, steadily. It is mesmerizing to watch them. "Like a ballet" is how someone described it in the newspaper recently. *Maybe,* I think. *But if it is, it is a strange and silent dance with death.*

I wonder how much longer I will be here. How much longer any of us will be here, raking, clearing, hoping, blessing, standing by, bearing witness. The end date for the recovery effort floats about in conversations. End of May? June? It is a curious feeling. When our work is done here, who will recover *us?* Who will look for us beneath the rubble of these months? Who will sift through the dirt searching for pieces of us, the bits and particles of who we were? Who will piece us back together; who will bless?

The night is just beginning, and there will be time for pondering such questions. The problem is we do not yet know we have been shattered. It's too early. We still think that we are the same people. We do not know that parts of us will be found on the tops of buildings, and in debris at Fresh Kills, and in manholes five years later. It is too early to know that every new discovery, no matter how many years later, no matter where we are, will break us a little. Every new bit recovered will prompt us to close our eyes and to whisper a prayer. We will look toward the heavens. We will see the bones before us. We will surround them with light. And, somewhere, ethereal men and women will remove their hats, bow their heads, and wait for the blessing that is sure to come.

11

REENTRY

I'M NOT SURE WHEN I stopped saying a prayer every time I saw an airplane, when I stopped squinting my eyes and extending my hand to give the illusion that I was holding the plane in my palm or balancing it on the tip of my finger, supporting it, guiding it. At some point, I must have stopped whispering, "Please, dear God, keep them aloft. Don't let them fall," but I couldn't tell you when. It used to be that I would look hard at every plane that crossed the sky, anxiously watching for any hint of trouble, expecting at any moment that it would take a treacherous and sudden turn—toward the city, toward the ground, toward certain death. I'm aware that I have stopped doing this, although an involuntary "Please, God, please," will still slip out every once in a while.

In the same way, I would shudder involuntarily every time I'd see a clump of leaves or debris on the side of the road as I drove. For a split second, I would be sure that I was seeing remains out of the corner of my eye. A discarded shoe or a scrap of muddy material would make me hit my brakes or jerk my head around. *What was that?* I would wonder. *Did I see something? Was that a torso? A limb? Is that decay I smell?* Strangely, I did not see human remains in animals killed along the road—these were recognizable—but I know that my heart sagged more than usual with each stiff raccoon or motionless squirrel I passed.

Now, years later, the dead I encounter are all intact, whole, known, and for the most part beloved by someone. The dead are those who have died on hospice, or whose funerals I have been asked to officiate. From time to time, the dead belong to my family. Death continues to come, but it is understandable, the dead recognizable. We usually know when and how they died; sometimes we are there. We can say our good-byes, we can bury them or cremate them, we can scatter their ashes, we can visit their graves. We can honor them one by one, which is enough to bear. Whether death comes as a result of disease or an accident, whether it is a suicide or a birth defect, most of us can eventually accept it.

What makes the deaths of September 11 so difficult is clearly the violent, communal, and very public way in which people perished, as well as the lack of recognizable remains. The world itself became unrecognizable on that beautiful blue morning. When the sky went black and the world went white with ash, it felt apocalyptic. Cultures, races, walks of life could hardly be distinguished. We watched them walk, shattered and bloodied, covered in debris and death. Shell-shocked and broken, all seemed to know that they themselves could be the ash that was covering their skin, their clothes, their identities, their spirits. Those who could, walked. They walked away from death. They walked toward life. They walked because there was nothing else to do but keep moving. And as they walked, they encountered the kindness and courage of strangers, reminding them of who they were, and of who they had been before the world went mad. But, at some point, they would have to stop moving, and that's when the thinking and the questioning—and the trauma—would really begin.

What do we do with those events for which there are no easy answers? In the months following the attacks of September 11, churches, synagogues, and houses of worship experienced a surge in attendance. People were looking for comfort, for hope, for an explanation to make sense of things, and they were looking in the places that stood for Order and Meaning. Who was in charge? If there was a God, how could He/She let this happen?

One of the most moving and poignant responses to the question of God's absence in the presence of suffering is recounted by Elie Wiesel in his autobiography, entitled *Night*. As he was forced to watch a young boy hang from the gallows of a concentration camp, dying a slow, torturous death, a prisoner in the crowd cried out: "Where is God now?" Wiesel writes, "And I heard a voice within me answer him: 'Where is He? Here He is—He is hanging here on this gallows.'"

Why do terrible things happen? Perhaps they happen not because God refuses to act in human history but because we refuse to act humanely. We are children running with expensive watches, with scissors, with the power to break and to hurt, to squander and to maim. We have the freedom to make terrible choices or to aspire toward holiness. And if we continue to point to the absence of God in the presence of evil, we will never take responsibility for our own actions, nor will we discover the God-ever-present, whose heart continues to break with ours.

Tragedy, heartbreak, illness, death—all of these place us squarely at the crossroads of existential and spiritual growth. What we do with the challenges that are sure to come is up to us. Most of us live our lives making deals with God or the Universe, consciously or unconsciously praying for answers to our prayers in exchange for the promise to do better, to be better, to try harder, to be more loving, more generous, more devoted. This is understandable, but it doesn't really get us anywhere in the long run, because some prayers will appear to get answered and some will not. The truth is that we are fragile, finite creatures. We get sick, we get injured, we hurt one another, we die. We fill our natural world, and our bodies, with toxins and wonder why there are more cancers, more illnesses. We hoard our wealth and our resources and wonder why there is resentment and violence. In essence, many of us go along just fine, without much thought about God or meaning, until the other shoe drops and we find ourselves in trouble, like a gambler who has played his last bad card.

I didn't contemplate the risks when I volunteered to serve at Ground Zero, though part of me must've known it was a gamble. None of us could have anticipated what was at stake or what it might mean later when forced to play the cards we were dealt. We simply came to that giant smoldering cavern of a table calling, *All in*. And, for some, it *was* all. For some, it cost them their lives due to 9/11-related illnesses; for others, their marriages or their mental health. Many paid with pieces of their hearts where sorrow would always remain. After blessing the parts of others, I paid with parts of myself, parts of my body.

A few years after completing my last shift at Ground Zero, I was diagnosed with cancer. I'd be lying if I didn't say it felt like a slap in the face. Not a very spiritually evolved reaction on my part, I admit. Wasn't God supposed to protect those of us who served . . . at least a little? I knew this kind of primitive thinking was never going to help me cope, nor would it honor those who'd suffered far worse fates. But it rose to the surface like the red imprint of a hand on my cheek. It took me awhile to understand that it was not God who smacked me; in fact, it wasn't a smack at all. It was simply the consequence of being human. Being shocked by my own mortality, my own fragile existence, meant that I needed to surrender to a deeper faith, one that didn't rely on life going well—even if it meant standing on a frightening precipice.

One of the first tests required before my surgery was a chest X-ray. The last time I'd had one had been years before in my old doctor's office. He was an attractive, kindly man who had been an Army doctor during the Korean War. Articles to that effect decorated his heavy wooden desk in frames and under glass. He believed a good shot of penicillin in the bum would cure just about anything; and a chest X-ray was the best way to tell if you had a bad cold or pneumonia. A lot of the time, he was right—but my friends used to tease me about the frequency with which I dropped my pants or exposed my breasts in his office. They said it was not normal. A chest X-ray at his office would entail baring my breasts and having him take the pictures. It was always horrifying to me, but I would comply, telling myself that he was, after all, a doctor.

This was going through my mind as I waited to be called for the X-ray after leaving Bernadette, my EKG technician, in the belly of the hospital. "Please let it be another woman. Please let it be another woman," I found myself chanting silently like a mantra. Just then, a lovely woman wearing a white lab coat and carrying a clipboard appeared. Her dark hair was smoothed back in a ponytail, her posture perfect, her manner poised. *Yes!* I thought with relief. But, strangely, the name she called did not resemble mine in the least. *This must be a mistake,* I argued to myself, because I had already started getting up out of my chair. She called it again. Determined as I was, I could not contort it to sound even remotely close. As I sat back down, a pleasant-looking, white-haired man rose to his feet (after a nudge from his wife). I forced the envy back down my throat, ashamed . . . but just barely.

After another minute or two, a young, handsome man appeared. "Andrea Raynor," he called. I blinked, adjusting to this reality like one whose hiding place has been exposed in a sudden flick of the light switch. My knee-jerk reaction was *Please, God, don't let him be the one to do the X-rays!* He was outgoing, friendly, and energetic—and way too attractive for me to feel comfortable about being half naked in front of him. *Okay, Lord, here we go,* I mumbled in my head. *Very funny. I get the joke. Learn to accept myself.* When you get the opposite of what you pray for, there's often a lesson buried in plain sight.

My smiling technician led me like a stable pony to the room with the X-ray machine. There was no sense in fighting it. *Just remember, you will never see this man again,* I said to myself, as if that would spare me the horror and embarrassment to come. I just could not get used to baring my breasts all the time to strangers. It brought up all my insecurities and feelings about my breasts. Pointing to a small closet, he instructed me, per usual, to strip from the waist up and to put the gown on—opened to the back.

"To the back?" I asked with surprise.

"Yep, that's right," he answered cheerfully. "To the back."

I felt a rush of relief. To the back. Could this mean that I would not be exposing my breasts? I mean, how could I if it was opened to the back, right? I put on the gown and stepped shyly out of the changing room.

"Okay then," he said breezily, clearly trying to put me at ease. "Let's get started."

He gently positioned me with my chest pressed against a panel. "Is this it?" I asked, surprised. "Does the X-ray come through this panel?"

"Oh no." He smiled, looking at me kindly, as one does with all simpletons. "The X-ray is taken through your back. See there," he said, pointing toward the wall behind me. "That is where it comes from. Just try to hold really still so I can get a good picture, okay?"

If he had asked me to stand there and recite the Pledge of Allegiance, I would have done so gladly. I became the model of stillness, a regular Zen master. My gratitude for having gotten

a reprieve from my self-hatred, or at least my self-conscious-
ness, outweighed the shame at having felt this in the first
place. *Must work on this*, I thought, making a mental note and
flinging it to the back of my brain.

It took only a few painless minutes to do the X-rays. When
they were done, my technician appeared, like the Great Oz,
from behind the wall—a wall that protects him from daily ex-
posure to radiation, a hazard of his job. "Want to see what
we've got?" he asked with an easy smile. "Let's make sure we
have a clear picture."

"Okay." I smiled back. He turned on a screen, and there,
in an instant, was a picture of what lies, every day, every minute, every pulsing second beneath the surface of my skin. I
looked at it—at me—in wonder. The technician began pointing out the various parts of my body, my ribs and clavicles,
and the pear-shaped outline of my heart. He was like a proud
father—adoring and energetic. He seemed genuinely excited
to share his knowledge, not caring whether I already knew the
information or not. That wasn't important. The point was that
he knew, and what he knew was more than anatomy. His en-
thusiasm and awe gave the impression that he was letting me
in on a great secret, namely that the body is a magnificent
thing, a vessel of mystery.

Many thoughts passed through my mind as I stood there
looking at the frame that holds me together. I thought of the
bodies, broken yet beautiful, that I had seen at Ground Zero. I
thought of the Spirit of Life, which swirls and pulsates invisi-
bly through these bones and tissues, through the organs and
cavities, and the blood that circulates in ever-constant rivers

through our veins. I beheld myself, as if from a short distance, like a painter who steps back to consider her work. The symmetry of my lungs, the slight curve at the base of my spine, the shadow of my heart resting like a mysterious sea creature in a cave—I observed all of this with quiet reverence. And then I felt a well of love and care begin to surface for my little self. It was almost as if I was standing outside of myself, outside of this particular life, and feeling tender and maternal toward the self that I now embody.

Whoever lives in that little frame can't be all bad, I thought. I wanted to tuck myself under my arm, to shield myself, and to take me straight home! This is the only body I have to live in. This delicate collection of tissue and bone. I am the only me there will ever be. This life is the only one I can know for sure. There is no guarantee about the future; there is only here and now. How do I want to live?

How? Tenderly. Respectfully. Aware of the finite nature of our existence. Open to mystery, to the unexpected ways in which the Divine comes to us. I want to live with ears open so that I can hear others calling me. I want to live with some semblance of forgiveness toward the self that continues to stumble and fall. Because, somewhere, buried under the myriad day-to-days of our existence, buried beneath our fear and our insecurities, hidden under the surface of our skin, is the pulsating force of Life, ancient, unknowable, mysterious, and constant.

If I could put my ear to my own heart, like one listening for the ocean in a shell, what would I hear? Would I hear the voice of God? Would the drumbeat of my heart make me turn my horse toward home? Like one straining to make out the

sound of words carried on the wind, I could only grasp fragments of meaning: Honor the Soul that lives in the body,
honor your own body and those of others; the intricacies of
the body point toward Mystery. And, finally: There is no sepa-
ration between the physical and the spiritual—there is only
and always the pulse of Life, swirling, moving, echoing, invisible, infusing all that is with something beyond our comprehension.

Listening to the whoosh and whisper of blood through the
heart, of oxygen through the lungs may be the first step toward
finding our way Home. And what is Home? Is it a feeling? Is it a
sense of belonging? A safe haven? Looking at my X-ray, I began
to understand that Home is rooted in a clear sense of who I am,
both as a spirit and as a body. We live in these bodies, but few of
us know who we are. The physical experience commands our attention—feed me, keep me warm, let me rest—but the Spiritual
Self is the North Star by which we chart our course. The way
will always be obscured if we fail to honor the Spirit within.

Perhaps this is why I always felt rising from the broken remains at Ground Zero was, strangely enough, a stubborn affirmation of life. The bones and tissues through which life had
pulsed gave quiet witness to the uniqueness of each person
who perished. DNA evidence meant finding an individual,
connecting to a life, like a needle weaving in and out of fabric
knit from the beginning of time. "Listen!" the bodies seem to
say. "Listen to the voices which rise from these ashes. Listen to
the Voice, still and small, within yourself. Listen, and you will
hear that nothing can alter the inherent beauty of life." Each of
us must look within to discover the beauty that is uniquely

ours; and, discovering it, we must seek to honor it by becoming who we were created to be.

Looking at my X-ray, I began to grasp how little I know of myself, how little I understand. Looking at my X-ray, I began to hear a voice whispering, "Go within. Go within . . . and discover who you are."

12

ALLIE-ALLIE-IN-COME-FREE

I am in God's presence night and day—
And he never turns his face away.

—WILLIAM BLAKE

IN THE DARKNESS, A child lies motionless, all senses heightened, every cell alive. Each beat of the heart pulsates beneath the surface of gossamer skin, the delicate rib cage rising and falling imperceptibly. The night air is alive and fragrant. It smells of earth and leaves, of moss and wood, and occasionally of some unseen kitchen's roast. The chirping of crickets is almost deafening. Sound is the only guardian; it is the one protection against being discovered. A voice in the distance, a rustle of leaves nearby map the battleground. And just when it seems like the heart can tolerate no more, when the silence has pressed itself too tightly against those ribs, comes the merciful ring of "Allie-allie-in-come-free! Allie-allie-in-come-free!" Rescue at last! Safety at last! The child springs like Lazarus from the tomb, from the purgatory of hiding, to run home, home, blessed home. Into the light, out of the darkness, free from the danger that lurks in the shadows, free from the terror of hiding alone.

I never liked hide-and-seek as a child, especially the way we played it in my neighborhood in Ohio. We called it Kick the Can. On warm summer nights, we would gather, choose the place for the can, choose home base, and set the boundaries for hiding. Someone would be It, everyone else would hide, and the game would begin. If you were found, you became a prisoner until someone was brave enough to storm the base and kick the can, setting you free. Then the quiet would be shattered by tin tumbling across concrete and by the happy shrieks of those who were released once more into the arms of the night.

The can was usually set up near our back porch because of the central location of our house. It sat at the base of a hill with a field to one side and woods to the other. Our playing area was fairly large, encompassing the several surrounding houses, which were separated by hills and trees and creeks. Most of the kids in the neighborhood found it very exciting; I, on the other hand, was terrified.

I never liked being It, never liked setting off into the night alone, heart pounding, wondering if someone was going to jump out and startle me. But I liked hiding even less. Although I enjoyed the thrill of feeling alive and independent, loved the balmy air, loved the way voices would carry, and the challenge of finding a good place to hide, I dreaded the waiting. I was terrified of the waiting, of the anticipation of being discovered, and, even worse, of the idea of being forgotten out there in the dark. If I was never found, would I win the game, or would I be lost forever?

I was good at hiding. I could stay still as a stone as the seeker passed dangerously near. Sometimes, when the silence and the darkness settled in too close around me, I would give myself away, preferring to be caught rather than be imprisoned by the night any longer. And if I did manage to remain hidden, I would strain my ears for the first sign of that blessed bellow: "Allie-allie-in-come-free!" Then I would run down the hill to my house, run toward the warm light of our little porch, and the familiar sound of my parents' voices drifting through the open windows. *I am found! I am found!* I would think. *I survived and I am home.* The porch light would keep the dark woods and the fields at bay while the surrounding houses glowed again like watchful sentries rather than menacing jack-o'-lanterns.

There have been many moments in my life when I have felt as if I were setting out into the darkness alone, setting out in search of whoever might be hiding, whoever might be waiting to be found, to be released from their isolation. This search has led me to the homeless who hide in plain sight before us; it has led me to the bedsides of the dying who wait for release; and it has brought me knee-deep in human remains. When you offer to be It for another human being, you commit yourself to the search, to the dogged task of finding and retrieving the lost, regardless of the possibility that they might not want to be found. You take the chance that, even if you guide someone to the safety of the porch light, they may choose to run headlong back into the woods, back into the darkness. That is not your concern. Your concern is only to keep searching, to keep calling, to keep the light within sight, and to listen.

The times I have hidden in my life are by far the more terrifying. Hiding, we cut ourselves off from the company of others; we decide that it is every person for himself or herself, that the odds are better if we go it alone, and that we will take our chances when it comes to being lost indefinitely. When we hide from ourselves or others, the light which used to signal home seems inaccessible; the voices once recognized as those of friends seem foreign or threatening.

Sometimes this happens with illness. When we, or someone we love, are diagnosed with an illness, especially a serious illness, we often feel like hiding. We don't want to talk about it. We don't want friends to ask us about it; and as we run, the world itself transforms into something dark and unrecognizable. Sometimes we strain our ears to hear if God is coming after us, coming to save us; and sometimes, we are terrified that the only response we will get is the sound of our own blood pumping in our ears.

How do we keep God alive in ourselves? How do we bear the things that happen, the things we cannot prevent? We keep moving, keep seeking; we come out of hiding, we listen for guidance, we open our eyes to the light ahead. We talk and we listen, and we sometimes do things that don't seem to make sense to others. The Norwegian novelist Johan Bojer describes something like this in his story "The Great Hunger." He writes:

An anti-social newcomer moved into the village and put a fence around his property with a sign saying, "Keep Out." He also put a vicious dog in the fence to keep anyone from climbing it. One day, the neighbor's little girl reached inside the fence to pet the dog and the dog grabbed her by the arm and savagely bit and killed her.

The townspeople were enraged and refused to speak to the recluse. They wouldn't sell him groceries at the store. When it came time for planting, they wouldn't sell him seed. The man became destitute and didn't know what to do. One day, he saw another man sowing seed on his field. He ran out and discovered it was the father of the little girl.

"Why are you doing this?" he asked.

The father replied, "I am doing this to keep God alive in me."

To KEEP GOD alive inside of us when hardship comes is a difficult task. At first, we may die a little inside. Sometimes the inner flame is nearly doused. But this need not be the end of our story. The man whose daughter was killed didn't pretend to forgive the recluse for his daughter's death; he didn't rush right over with a fruit basket or feign some noble acceptance of God's will. No. He watched the townspeople reject this man. He stood by as they forced him into near starvation by not selling him groceries or even seed. The father didn't protest this treatment. On the contrary, his silence spoke volumes about his approval.

Then something happened to him; something happened within him. He realized that each day he spent embittered, each day he lived with hatred seeping into the cracks of his shattered heart, each day he refused to do what he would normally do, namely to show compassion to another person, he died a little more inside. He could not bring his daughter back to life, but he could begin to live again himself. And he did this by the simple act of sowing seed on the field of one who was in need, even though this one was the source of his anguish. With each handful of seed tossed, the flame began to burn again inside of him. With each row of planting completed, he moved toward something that resembled his life among the living.

God, hope, joy, ultimate meaning, inner happiness, whatever you might call it dies a little in us each day that we choose to hide, choose to cut ourselves off, choose to stop caring about the rest of humanity. And we die. Events like 9/11, like children dying of starvation, like people freezing on the streets of the most affluent cities in the world, these events press into us. They force the heart into hiding because the fear of pain is so great. We become overwhelmed, numb, and our sense of self-protection is ignited. We do not want to see or feel or hear. But if we are willing to open our eyes, we will find God seeking us; if we open our ears, we will hear God calling us—and we can follow that Voice, which beacons us toward the light, toward the best of who we are.

I am reminded of Dr. Viktor Frankl, the Austrian psychiatrist and Holocaust survivor. He witnessed murder and experienced cruelty beyond comprehension. He was stripped of his dignity, deprived of his humanity, starved and beaten, yet was still somehow able to experience meaning, still able to feel something like blessing. While working in a trench and feeling that death might be imminent, he described the following:

> The dawn was grey around us; grey was the sky above; grey the snow in the pale light of dawn; grey the rags in which my fellow prisoners were clad, and grey their faces. I was again conversing silently with my wife, or perhaps I was struggling to find the *reason* for my sufferings, my slow dying. In a last violent protest against the hopelessness of imminent death, I sensed my spirit piercing through the enveloping gloom. I felt it transcend that hopeless, meaningless world, and from somewhere I heard a victorious "Yes" in answer to my question of the existence of an ultimate purpose. At that moment, a light was lit in a distant farmhouse, which stood on the horizon as if painted there, in the midst of the miserable grey of a dawning morning in Bavaria. *"Et lux in tenebris lucet"*—and the light shineth in the darkness.*

WE ARE HERE to be lights in the darkness. We are here to seek others and to be found ourselves. Keep asking. Keep knocking. Keep calling in the night. Keep listening. God is present.

* Viktor Frankl, *Man's Search for Meaning*, pp. 51–52.

AUTHOR NOTE

I will always feel honored to have served at Ground Zero. Many others are now gone, having succumbed to 9/11-related illnesses. I was fortunate to have survived my cancer, as well as the sorrow of a miscarriage suffered not long after my service concluded. Whether this loss was a direct result of the time spent at Ground Zero, I will never know—but in my heart, they will always be connected.

I continue to pray for families devastated by loss and for all who bear the scars of sorrow. Families like the Lewises. Adam Lewis was thirty-six-years old when he was killed at the World Trade Center, leaving the love of his life, Patty, to care for their four children. Reilly, the oldest, was only eight years old. She and my daughter met in college and became fast friends. Through the years, I sometimes wondered if I'd blessed a part of her dad.

With respect and gratitude, I remember the Foley brothers, Tommy and Danny. Tommy, thirty-two, was a decorated veteran of the FDNY. He died when the towers collapsed. His brother Danny, also a firefighter, spent ten days searching for his brother until, miraculously, he found him in the wreckage. Then he returned again and again to search for others. He was forty-six when he died from pancreatic cancer related to the rescue and recovery efforts, leaving behind his wife, Carrie, and their five children.

To remember those who lived and worked and served, those who died and those who survived is a sacred responsibility. By remembering, we keep a part of them here with us. We keep them close. It is a tangible eternity that unspools with our stories and our laughter. We are all in this together.

ACKNOWLEDGMENTS

Heartfelt thanks to Libby McGuire, Suzanne Donahue, and the people at Atria Books for giving these stories new wings in honor of the twentieth anniversary of September 11. And thanks, always, to my brilliant editor, Peter Borland, who first helped me shape and sharpen them as part of *The Voice That Calls You Home*.

Thank you to my family for your support and for bearing with me through the years. Andrew, Cat, and Alex, you are the lights of my life. Mom, you remain the safe shore.

Finally, endless waves of gratitude to my indomitable agent, Cynthia Manson, who envisioned this book twenty years ago and has been its champion ever since. It was you who first urged me to remember and to write about my shifts at Ground Zero. Without your tireless efforts and faith in me, these stories might have been lost to time. Thank you, Cynthia. I feel the angels smiling.

ABOUT THE AUTHOR

Andrea Raynor, a graduate of Harvard Divinity School, served as a hospice chaplain and spiritual counselor for more than twenty years. A United Methodist minister, she has worked with the homeless in New York City and Boston, and was a pastor to churches in New York, Connecticut, and Massachusetts. In the aftermath of September 11, she served as a chaplain to the temporary morgue at Ground Zero, offering blessings over remains and support to the many workers on-site. Her books include *The Voice That Calls You Home: Inspiration for Life's Journeys*; *Incognito: Lost and Found at Harvard Divinity School*; *A Light on the Corner: Discovering the Sacred in the Everyday*; *The Alphabet of Grief: Words to Help in Times of Sorrow*; and a short story titled, "The Choice." She has lectured throughout the country and has appeared as a guest on public television and radio. She lives in Rye, New York, where she is also the chaplain to the fire department.

Photos were not allowed to be taken during the initial search and rescue phase at Ground Zero. Only months later, when it was clearly a recovery and not a rescue effort, was it deemed okay. Still, I didn't feel entirely comfortable, and only took these few photos with a disposable camera.

Taking our children, Cat and Alex, to NYC on 9/22/01
to reassure them the city was still strong and standing.

With Rev. Lyndon Harris at St. Paul's Chapel, which (under his direction) became a respite center for workers and volunteers at Ground Zero.

Inside St. Paul's with fellow
workers and volunteers.
Together, we kept our spirits up.

The Deutsche Bank, severely damaged.

Sometimes I hitched a ride with other workers to get around the site.
Looking at these young faces, I often thought of those who did not survive.

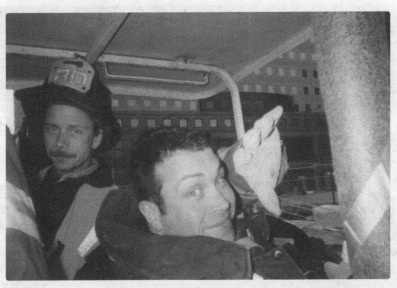

More faces of those who bravely served at Ground Zero.

My first ID badge issued by
the Red Cross in November.

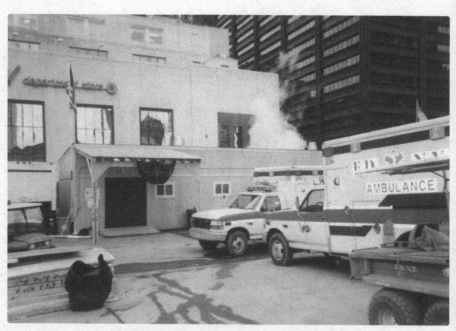

The Temporary Mortuary, where bodies and fragments
of bodies were brought when they were recovered.

Close-up of the door.

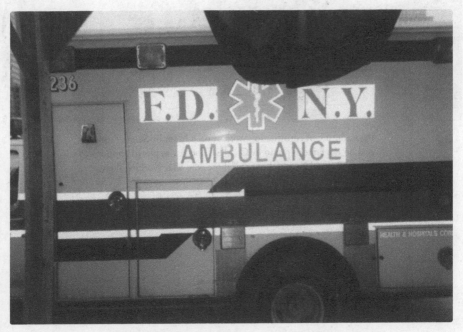

An ambulance waits outside the temporary morgue.

The sculpture of construction workers on a beam by Sergio Furnari (based on the famous photo by Charles Ebbets) was placed temporarily near Ground Zero to honor all those who were working there.

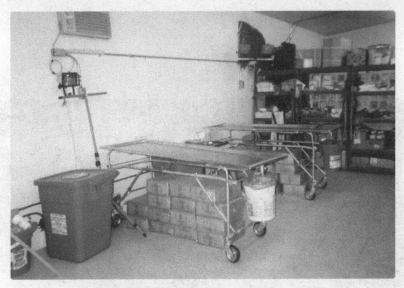

Inside the temporary mortuary, where remains were
brought, recorded, identified if possible, and blessed.

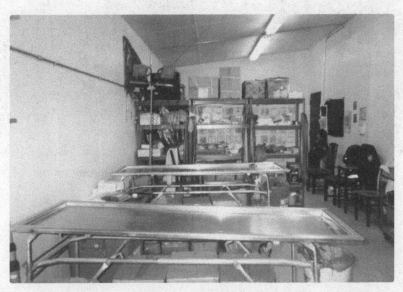

Another view of the mortuary interior. The folding chairs on the right are
where we, who were assigned there, spent many long hours waiting for remains.

The rescue dogs at Ground Zero eventually became therapy
dogs for those who served. Their presence was a comfort.

Surveying the site from the roof of Station 10–10.

Celebrating Communion on Palm Sunday with Fr. Brian Jordan, a Franciscan priest.

The "Pile" became the "Pit."

I wish I could remember this sergeant's name. This was captured on his last day at Ground Zero after nearly a year of service. I pray he is still healthy and well.

My last badge, taken for the Recovery Ceremony. The look in my eyes shows the accumulated sorrow of those months.

Standing in front of the last beam taken down at Ground Zero, now at the 9/11 Museum.

I will always cherish this 9/11 T-Mort Chaplain pin,
which I wear on my Rye Fire Department jacket.